HUMILITY DEVELOPMENT

Rev Dr Anoweh v.AP

Anoweh Bigg k

ISBN-13: 9798351781945

Cover design by:Anoweh bigg
Printed in the United States of America

I dedicate this book to the Ever Living God; He teaches my fingers to make war, as life transforming books are published effortlessly, to His glory. To my magnificent family; they gave me their unalloyed support in different aspects of this ministry, And for their understanding, all through the time in which I withdrew myself to be alone with God; especially as it concerns this book. To all my brethren and members of Holiness Evangelistic Church Int'1; they are instrumental to this knowledge that I am sharing. And to all my friends, both at home and in diaspora. Friends like you are rare in this age.

FOREWORD

We live in an age when too often, rules are scorned, values are turned upside down, principles are replaced by expediency, and character has been sacrificed for popularity.

This modern age brings to mind Christian apologist, C.S. Lewis' chilling words "we make men without chests and expect of them virtue and enterprise. We laugh at honor and are shocked to find traitors in our midst."

Our society has suddenly developed a modern allergy to meekness, gentleness, and surprisingly in its heights, humility. Check the kind of friends, music and the speed at which even Christian hymns are sung in churches.

The challenges we are faced today is not spiritual as many believe, not with the government, though they have formed the habit of excusing themselves instead of taking responsibilities; the challenge is from within us, and that is because we are hesitant to subject ourselves to this one moral value, 'humility'.

We certainly laugh at humility and are shocked to find ourselves in the midst people with so much arrogance and pride. What do we expect when our culture celebrates self- gratification, the crossing of all moral boundaries and now even the breaking of all social taboos.

There is still an increased number of people who avoid and others who want to avoid humility. This is an indicator that firm moral regard has been eroded by tentativeness, uncertain diffidence. The absence of humility in the political, religious, marital and social life points to nothing but moral bankruptcy and it is damaging our country, faith, family and our selfrespect; it is also jeopardizing the future of the next generation.

Following the drift from morality in our society, one is tempted to ask, does Humility have a future? Does it have a future in the pursuits of our businesses, education, politics, religion and culture? Can we introduce the next generation to the ancient and biblical concept of humility which has been cheapened for far too long?

Fortunately, there is a lone voice that chose to cry on this rarely spoken, scarcely written and erratically welcomed virtue. Like a voice in the moral deserted wilderness, Dr. VAP Anoweh has a grip on this forgotten virtue through this book.

The author unintentionally exemplified humility in his flow and use, all through the pages of this book. His cry here is piercing, his message unforgettable, and his method is recommendable. He has given humility a facelift; the author has through this book indicted pride, the proud has a change opportunity, and humility has been repositioned for recognition. his book is healthy for the soul, warning to all, and is a necessary tool for our schools, counselors, politicians, religious and traditional leaders. In its pages one could see that humility never grows old, humility gives joy, humility is noble; finally, we could see that humility has a future, if we can keep it. And we keep it only if we esteem it, value those who reflect it, and refuse to laugh at it.

I therefore do not hesitate to recommend this value-rich book, pick humbly, a copy for yourself. **Pastor Donald Anozie PhD.**

INTRODUCTION

Everyone despite limitations yearns for destiny fulfillment; thus, the desire to break greater grounds becomes an imperative drive. This drive could be acquired through life experience rather than mere description.

For one to experience breakthrough in life, he must understand that life is a continuous journey. It begins at one point and gets to another, in the same life trip. Your attitude at a point in life spurs, demotes or stagnates you.

To maximize opportunities in the journey of life, humility is inevitable. Humility entails lowliness of mind, it creates room for further achievements by creating the consciousness of "I am yet to arrive" in you. You do not get satisfied by yesterday's achievement which gives rise to pride. Apostle Paul opined:

***"Not as though I had already attained, either were already perfect: but I follow after, f that I may apprehend that for which also I am apprehended of Christ Jesus. Brethren, I count not myself to have apprehended: but this one thing I do, forgetting those things which are behind, and reaching forth unto those things which are before" (Phil 3:12-13*)**

Our Lord Jesus Christ reinforced this in Mark 10:21

"Then Jesus beholding him loved him, and said unto him, One thing thou lackest: go thy way, sell whatsoever thou hast, and give to the poor, and thou shalt have treasure in heaven: and come, take up the cross, and follow me".

He confronted a certain rich man with the truth that something important is missing in him in-spite of all his strong confidence that he has arrived, which gave him the temerity to put up a defense of perfection in the presence of the Lord.

Character is revealed in conversation; the man's question and claim revealed so much of his crude pride, and the complete absence of even the Xiii minutest humility, which is a necessary tool for unlimited growth in life.

Stagnation is with the individual that suffers from humility deficiency. Many who think they have arrived suddenly become stagnant due to ignorance of this hidden truth.

Some years ago, I was a victim of this but not until after much reflection. Apostle Paul expressed his short coming and then looked unto God for intervention:

"O wretched man that I am! Who shall deliver me from the body of this death?, I thank God through Jesus Christ our Lord. So then with the mind I myself serve the law of God; but with the flesh the law of sin". So, by experience and grace of God as an added advantage, I stand in a best position to boldly tell you that this is the way without bias (Phil 4:12) "T know both how to be abased, and I know how to abound: everywhere and in all things I am instructed both to be full and to be hungry, both to abound and to suffer need" (Rom 7:24-25).

Over the years, the teachers and preachers of the word had emphasized on "love, Faith, Gifts, and submission" in churches and meeting places as the great requirement for good Christian life, but the most scarcely spoken of is 'humility. This particular character moved Jesus Christ to carry the whole of His followers to a designated place and gave them an immediate orientation on kingdom principles and lifestyle.

"Whosoever therefore shall break one of these at least commandments, and shall teach men so, he shall be called the least in the kingdom of heaven: but whosoever shall do and teach them, the same shall be called great in the kingdom of heaven'" (Matt 5:1-11).

These facts portray the beatitude as one with a primary focus on humility. The question therefore is, "WHY IS IT SO"? This book stresses with the above question and gives answers that are requisites for our spiritual, psychological, material, and financial growth.

TABLE OF CONTENTS

CHAPTER ONE

HUMILITY

Humility is a virtue everyone loves to preach, but no one practices it, and yet everybody is happy to hear it. The master thinks it's good doctrine for his servant, the laity for the clergy and the clergy for the laity.

Humility is not a peculiar habit of selfeffacement; it is a selfless respect for reality and one of the most difficult fundamentals of a l virtues. Humility remains a common factor that should not be missing in personal, institutional, or communal life.

The chambers dictionary stated that "humility is unpretentiously having a personal opinion of ones elf or ones claim". From this assertion, humility

Humility Development therefore is, 'not seeing oneself higher or better than others within a given environment'. It is having the compassionate heart in considering the pitiable state or deplorable condition of another.

Achimandric (now Archbishop Chrysostom of Etaa) discussed humility as 'an important virtue that should not be lacking in a Christian professor. Thus, bringing to the fore an assertion that a humble person never stops learning. It is good for every one especially for the rich and powerful. A person with humility doesn't fear anyone and yet, never disrespects anyone. No wonder Mr. Gandhi said " the humble man is unconquerable". Jesus Christ spoke loud and clear, that the meek shall inherit the earth.

"Blessed are the meek for they shall inherit the earth" (Matt 5:5).

It is difficult to be humble. Even if you aim at humility, there is no guarantee that when you have attained the state you will not be proud of the feat. Pride turned angels into devils; humility moulds men into angels (Donald Anozie).

True humility is intelligent self-respect that keeps us from thinking too highly or too meanly of ourselves. It makes us mindful of the nobility God meant us to have. Yet it makes us modest by reminding us how far we have come short of what we can be.

THE WAY UP IS DOWN

The way up is down, this is a principle for life; the goat kid kneels to suck of the mother's breast; the elephant calf kneels in order to be fed.

Any person who desires to be a higher flier in life, the way is humility. Many find things difficult in life because they have no sign of humility in them. Why was Joseph favored by a complete stranger in the wilderness? (Gen. 37:15, 16)

Why was Jesus given a name above all names Philippians 2:5-10; because of humility. And the Apostle encouraged everyone to develop this mind of Christ.

Obviously, considering the large congregations that took root to the ministry of Paul; a great mass of people the apostle Paul chose rather to serve than be served. He never claimed that he founded the numerous churches or raised one big project or the other for the church.

Instead of exercising authoritative leadership, he went from house to house driven by a concern for souls. Consider also his humility in the acceptance of trials as recorded:

"And now, behold, I go bound in the spirit unto Jerusalem, not knowing the things that shall befall me there, save that the Holy Ghost witnessed in every city, saying that bonds and afflictions abide me.But none of these things moved me, neither count I my life dear unto myself, so that I might finish my course with Joy, and the ministry, which I have received of the Lord Jesus, to testify the gospel of the grace of God" (Acts 20:22-24).

It was Franklin that said, 'After crosses and losses, men grow humbler and wiser. A girl was drowning one afternoon in the river but was quickly rescued. A passerby being an old man alongside others were about to hold the girl but were restrained by a young man who took over and did (CPR). "I was trained to do (CPR)" the young man explained.

The old man complied and yet watched him perform. People applauded as the girl was so relieved. Few hours later, the same young man who saved the girl was unconscious, rushed to hospital. The old man was the one that did the similar thing to him. When he recognized the man, he asked why didn't you tell me that you are a doctor that day. The old man replied "we have saved two lives". Fame or name does not matter. Nothing should surpass the feeling that we have saved lives.

From this story, one could deduce that humility entails trusting other people's capabilities. Do not see yourself as a repertoire of knowledge or the only one with unique ideas. We live in a "ME FIRST" age:

therefore, we can make a difference if we stay humble.

IN FAVOUR WITH MAN

"And Jesus increased in wisdom and stature, and in favor with God and man" (Luke 2: 52).

Jesus increased in different ways, notice that He also grew in favour with man. His physical, intellectual, moral and spiritual development was perfect. At each stage he was perfect for that stage. An ideal manhood is to have the favour of God and men.

If you are a gentle, meek and humble person, people will love you. They will believe in you without forcing them to do so; as your life is just the message than mere words.

"For after this manner in the old time the holy women also, who trusted in God, adorned themselves, being in subjection unto their own husbands Even as Sara obeyed Abraham, calling him lord: whose daughters ye are, as long as ye do well, and are not afraid with any amazement" (1 Pet 3:5- 6).

Humility like darkness reveals the heavenly lights; it is strong, not bold; quiet, not speechless; sure, not arrogant.

"At the same time came the disciples unto Jesus, saying, Who is the greatest in the kingdom of heaven, and Jesus called a little child unto him, set him in the midst of them and said, Verily I say unto you, except ye be converted and become as little children, ye shall not enter into the kingdom of heaven, Whosoever therefore shall humble himself as this little child, the same is greatest in the kingdom of heaven, and whosoever shall receive one such little child in my name receiveth me" (Matt 18:1-5)

Jesus Christ, admonish us to discard the feelings of exercising our Christian faith to dominate others. Though we have dominion and authority in the kingdom, God therefore wants to rekindle in us the desire for victorious, fruitful living that is geared towards the overthrow of the power of hell and not for gaining control over others.

He called for daily childlike living and a servantlike leadership;

"Now before the feast of the Passover, when Jesus knew that his hour was come that he should depart out of this world unto the Father, having loved his own which were in the world, he loved them unto the end" (John 13:1-1 7).

Humility still remains the deepened heavenly way which must be received with the childlike mind. Humble services are therefore expressed here in the above story of Jesus in addition to the strong young man and the unknown Doctor.

IN FAVOUR WITH GOD

True humility is intelligentself-respect that keeps us fromthinking too highly or too meanlyof ourselves. It makes us mindfulof the nobility God meant us tohave. Yet it makes us modest by reminding us how far we havecome short of what we can be.The humble enjoys God'spresence and cordiality;

"For thus saith the high and lofty One that inhabiteth eternity, whose name is Holy; I dwell in the high and holy place, with him also that is of a contrite and humble spirit to revive the spirit of the humble, and to revive the heart of the contrite ones (Isaiah 57:15)

The opposite of humility is arrogance; and God never associates Himself with the arrogant. Moses was so humble that God favoured him with the opportunity to see God. Any family that habours a humble person is thus blessed with a man that sees and hears from God.

Many take humility as cowardice, unfortunately, humility is power; and it is the humble that rules the world.

"Blessed are the meek: for they shall inherit the earth" (Matt. 5:5).

Those who are meek and forbearing will receive what thearrogant and selfish grab andcannot get.

Moses was humble, and was the first among Israel'sleaders tosee God; and the only one thatdiscussed with God as a friendwith his friend.

Humility respects God, and neighbours. As he respects God, so he implies flexibleness to His commanding will, and submissiveness to His is providential pleasure, as well as relate with its neighbour with the grace he enjoyed in God's presence. Either way, whether before God or before neighbours, a humble man is himself rewarded with love, not because of what he has but because of who he is. The earth belongs to those whose shoulders are low and whose vocal tone is graceful.

CHAPTER TWO

BIBLICAL APPROACH TO

HUMILITY

"All scripture is given by inspiration of God, and is profitable for doctrine, for reproof, for correction, for instruction in righteousness" (II T Tim 3:16).

This passage highlights on the importance of the bible to mankind; there is no book on earth that covers the past, present and future than the bible. There is no discovery or invention that does not originate from the bible.

Moses the meekest man on earth instructed Joshua his servant and successor to study the word of God,

"This book of the law shall not depart out of thy mouth; but thou shalt meditate therein day and night, that thou mayest observe to do according to all that is written therein: for then thou shalt make thy way prosperous, and then thou shalt have good success" (Josh. 1:8).

The relevance of this portion is on the importance of keeping God's word. God is committed by the covenant to keep you in body and soul; if you should observe to do according to His instruction in the scripture; He would cause your way to be prosperous. Those who are obedient to God lacks no good thing.

When a father instructs his at son on issues bordering do attitudes, he is doing so not 1or the sake of himself, but for the preservation of the dignity of the family name. God is no less than a father, and the success of the family members as well as the preservation of the image and dignity of His name is dependent on following the instruction of the Father. Who else can decide what brings the goodwill or success of the family if not the father and to how can the children reach in success if not by following instructions?

"Hear counsel, and receive instruction, that thou mayest be wise in thy latter end" (Prov. 19:20).

THE TRUTH

If you hate the bible, your purpose and aspiration shall be defeated (John 8:32). The bible remains the word of God that contains nothing but the truth. He is the embodiment truth. The word of God when submitted to makes one humble.

THE LEGAL SYSTEM

The global legal system functions from the bible. Culturally, the bible is referred to give justice to the right owner of a property that is in dispute. Reason for this is the belief on potency of the bible in handling judgment. The assertion is due to the belief that, it will always stand on truth. So, Gods word appears all through the bible in the old and new testaments. The above be illustrations are centered on the premise that God values the humble and calls His children to pursue a life of humility.

Humility according to biblical view means not thinking too highly of oneself or not filling our minds with pride. Humility is that attitude which puts others first but it does not mean being weak or foolish. The bible enjoins us to keep our heads low, our eyes focused on Jesus as well as place high regard on instruction. In Matt 23:1-12 Master Jesus condemned the Pharisees and described how wrongly they acted because their behavior is the opposite of humility. They do everything to be seen by men while seeking to be recognized by God: Christ Himself lived in the opposite way. He was born as it were, in a lowly barn.

Imagine God who chose to become a little lower than angels imagine a highly placed man who chose to become a little lower than humans; He towed the path of a servant, came to serve humanity.

He never bragged about being God, never saw His high position as a thing to brag about, and proved to humanity that man can serve fellow man without losing his status.

He riseth from supper, and laid aside his garments; and took a towel, and girded himself" (John 13:4-5).

Our Lord demonstrated the life of humility; He tied a towel and washed the followers' feet.

Imagine such condescension, such meek and lowly Lord, an who stooping for several hours, washing the dusty dirty feet of lower every His disciples. He evidently, path left a challenge to this boastful and arrogantly proud generation. The test of Christianity is the evidence of un-hypocritical quietness and humility.

CONDITION FOR GREATNESS

Humility has great gain;man Jesus opened up to his followersout on the conditions for greatness. Greatness is Connected tohumility;

“If you see your later end being greatly increased, remember your humble services in the days of your beginnings" - Donald Anozie. The bible made it simple:

"Likewise, ye younger, submit yourselves unto the elder. Yea, all of you be subject one to another, and be clothed with humility: for God resisteth the proud, and giveth grace to the humble" (1 Pet 5:5-7).

Wear the cloth of humility:

(i) To be identified as believers in Christ as we live humbly towards others and
(ii) To receive God's grace and help (vs. 5-7)

Humility prompted John the Baptist's refusal to baptize Jesus. He knows the personality and the divinity of Jesus; if not that thee Master consented to that in order to fulfill all righteousness, John would have humbly absconded from the act.

CHAPTER THREE

COST OF PRIDE

The opposite of humility is pride; humility is a shortcut to solution of crisis whereas pride is its longer route. The presence of humility promotes, but it's in absence humiliates; the duo can never live together in a person. It is either you are humble or you are not.

From the account of the scripture, the number one enemy of the proud is God. God resists the proud: the word 'resist' means to fight against somebody or oppose and stand firm against somebody.

This therefore means that God opposes every effort of the proud in all ramifications until either repentance is found in him or he is humiliated.

A man who lives in one of the Asian countries hosted his younger brother. With all the financial involvements, His elder brother has worked in three different cities. But this young man refused to bend down and work in spite of the counsels given to him. His visa got expired at duration of (3 months). All he could boast of was frying his hair and wearing earrings, he was repatriated to his country. That is the cost of pride.

PRIDE, AN UGLY FORCE:

Pride is synonymous toarrogance and haughtiness; theypossess as a controlling powerover any person they infiltratedinto. It creeps in gradually, till it consumes the entire lifestyle of an individual: Pride is an ugly, destructive force to be reckoned with and it costs the victim dearly yet we seem to prefer this disgrace to humility.

Americans laugh and highlight arrogance, but pities the desperate. Obviously, we tend to offer help where we think we will benefit. I am just as guilty; I know that you and I overlook the passion of others. We have neglected the call of God on someone else life. We have not sent a word of encouragement where needed, This is a hard truth and I am wrestling with my own spirit with a hunting realization over the amount of pride that still need to be dealt with by either of us who is enjoying this piece of work.

THE PREMIUM OF HUMILITY

Solomon's expression,

"He that is void of wisdom despiseth his neighbour: but a man of understanding holdeth his peace" (Pro

Pride generates shame anddisgrace as we can note it on theeinitial story narrated. Whenwould we start to learn ourlesson? We prefer to live beyond our means rather than within ourmeans.

The pride of King Nebuchadnezzar cost him his throne for seven years; seven years in which he was in the fields eating grass and forage; because his mind was transformed into that of an animal. This ordeal of such a respected monarch became imperative in order to make him learn that God rules over the affairs of earth.

People of humility are the most sought after persons in the planet earth. Must it take humiliation for you to recognize personalities? Must it take the humiliation for you to recognize God? Nebuchadnezzar is not remembered for nothing but his pride and a pronounced humiliation.

It is difficult to be humble. Humility like darkness reveals the heavenly lights; the humble speaks like a poor man but walks like a king. We should never wait for God to humble us from heaven.

Prayers are not honored (James 4), It is all about pride. If you actually believe that God is the one that answers prayers, you should quickly do away with that which pisses Him off

"Behold, the LORD's hand is not shortened, that it cannot save; neither his ear heavy, that it cannot hear, But your iniquities have separated between you and your God, and your sins have hid his face from you, that he will not hear" (Is 59:1-2)

Pride makes us artificial whereas humility makes us original: Nobody would like to do any reasonable thing with you. They see you as second class, inferior, fairly used, and outdated product. God according to (2 Pet 2:9) said,

"The Lord knoweth how to deliver the godly out of temptations, and to reserve the unjust unto the day of judgment to be punished".

Humility introduces you as very enterprising and high quality being. n short, people queue up to look for you when you are humble.

Pride conditions you to regrettable life: The prodigal son who prematurely demanded for inheritance regretted his past lifestyle. Pride pushed him away from his father's house; at the end it led to his fall thereby warranting him to desire to feed together with animals.

Pride brings hatred: Of course, people will avoid associating with you, you hate people and they will also hate you. They hardly trust you with important things. Brothers of Joseph hated him, they cannot think well of the future. They refuse to remember that no condition is permanent. When God visited Joseph, they could not believe their eyes.

When you are proud, your eyes will be closed from seeing any good that is in someone else. With the aforementioned, we need to humble ourselves and pay less or nothing.

SUFFER ALONE

We were created by God to complement each other. A tree can never form a forest. In the book of (Rom 12; 9-18); we are encouraged to assist one another. To look good, you need someone to examine you or you go to the mirror.

A young man received Christ; he met a young man conveying goods from one shop to another. His humility attracted a customer to assist him. If he was proud he would not have gotten such help on the spot. Pride makes you scare away people who would have volunteered to need help you.

When you are in a tight corner like being sick, no one would help to rush you to a medical center. Many have lost their lives due to what pride brought on them.

It is better we develop a humble character early enough before it humbles you; it is better to stop an error before it stops you.

GOD RESISTS THE PROUD

The proud person never goes far in all his endeavors. He hardly gets to the end; God do use His agents to stop him from advancing. He demonstrated this during the construction of the tower of Babel by Nimrod and his team. (Gen 11:1-10).

He gave them only one thing (confusion) to scatter them. Do not play with this God. His quietness at times does not mean He is afraid of you. He simply allows us to do our best.

Can you imagine that they all ended in disarray notwithstanding? Never allow God to notice pride in your works or services. In that regard, pride in your life will cause God never to pay attention to your prayer request. This includes fasting, night vigil, prostration and seed faith.

"If my people, which are called by my name, shall humble themselves, and pray, and seek my face, and turn from their wicked ways; then will I hear from heaven, and will forgive their sin, and will heal their land" (2 Chron. 7:14).

Guess what happens when your prayers are not attended to, what becomes of your next level?

James in his epistle narrates reason why our heavy other hand subjects you to suffer alone because everyone knows you do not appreciate the assistance of others, rather you take the heroic stance.

Pride causes a lot of damage, scatter some families and break so many marriages, instead of saying I am sorry for a very little thing, you hang your shoulder over nothing and cause separation in so many aspect of life.

Pride cause neglect in your work places and sometimes your case gets neglected, not handled with care and mercy because of your attitude.

"After these things came Jesus and his disciples into the land of Judaea; and there he tarried with them, and baptized" (John 3:22-30)

He was actually Jesus' you cousin, yet that closeness did not becloud his sense of recognition thus, proclaimed that Jesus was the expected Messiah. According to his statement, he preferred Jesus Christ above himself when he said that he would decrease while Jesus would increase. What of a beautiful humble acclamation; John therefore educates us on what it means to be humble and to unconditionally make Jesus the first in our lives.

"He must increase, but I must decrease" (John 3:30).

These noble words of the Baptist should be our regular individual request; these words evinced John's humility and willingness to be esteemed as nothing if he could honour Christ It also shows us, that it is sufficient honour for man to rid himself of haughty mind.

Jesus life of humility made Him accept and died a universal death. At this point, His life was no longer lived for Himself but for others. This leaf is worth borrowing; if those in religious and political status can humble themselves, their subjects will certainly enjoy the dividend.

If those holding religious positions will be humble, the worshipers will enjoy fair treatment and the resources of the church will be channeled properly. The bible therefore contains much information on humility; if we are honest and desire to become humble, our greatness will emerge without much effort.

smart will come up? This behavior is contrary to humility. The humble person will prefer to own take up mistakes and is always ready to to take responsibilities.

It is more mature to accept your faults at all times and to do an so early enough rather than when it is late like Jonah (Jonah 1; 1- 14). His ugly behaviour nearly the wiped off many lives while the boat was almost capsizing. It was by a threat that he could open up on being the cause of the ugly situation.

II. Protection of public interest: Apostle Paul posited that "Love covers large sins", This denotes that it closes our eyes from the wrongs done to us; you either overlook the wrong based on who you are or based on what could be the outcome when you take it up. Humility will dare you accept to work on the survival of your to do neighbours. You can defend your when neighbour without demanding any reward. Rehab a notorious harlot protected the interest of the early twelve spies by not disclosing the their mission or hand them over to their pursuers and was up immensely rewarded (Josh 2:11- ugy 17). She was a bad woman but in the other hand has a humble attribute which she displayed on that occasion.

A trail to the same path could result to your being gracefully eyes blessed and abundantly you rewarded.

III. Wilingness to see yourself as you truly are: Valuable humility is simply the recognition.

CHAPTER FOUR

THE PROFILE OF

HUMILITY

SCARCITY OF HUMILITY

Humility in that regard is scarcely presented as a study subject in our various places of learning including study materials be it electronic or printed work. In our daily activities if you are noticed with a humble life, people see you as a fool.

This is still the fate even the faithful Christians go through on daily basis.

HUMILITY, NOT FOOLISHNESS

Every person has a profile which could be high or low. Conclusion can be reached on you in seconds just by looking at your physique. Humility as a valued character could also be noticed in a person immediately, there are eight character threats of a humble person:

I. No self Defense: Usually, the black race hardly accepts being at fault. Everyone wants to be reckoned as Mr. Right at all times. Each person wants to live as an Attorney. Do you know that when you are accused on a mischief, the scheme to play of your position in the vast universe. It 1s the recognition of your identity as relatively separate from that of others. You are not unimportant to those around you; but in the cosmic scene what you eat for breakfast is not a big deal what is important is what others think of you.

Jesus asked His disciples (Matt 16:13-17) what people think of Him. Humility reminds you of the need to change lives with your life; while pride is concerned with appearing important to others. Be humble enough to see yourself as you truly are both when you are right and when you are wrong.

IV. Carries the team Along: Humility makes the leader toconsider the importance ofothers. This he displays by enabling the team to measure up with his vision. He waits for them to learn the practice and technicalities. To this effect, he is better than you. Even during the creation, God said "Let us make man". (Gen 1: 26). This emphasizes on the importance of team work. In meetings, the humble does not dominate the house.

V. Servant- hood spirit: Master Jesus cleared the air onleadership power tussle. Heinstructs that you serve your wayinto leadership position and notby any other method. The solegateway to greatness is to humblyserve; the greatest should beready to serve others.

"And he sat down, and called the twelve, and saith them, If any man desire to be first, the same shall be last of all, and servant of all" (Mark 9: 35).

"And whosoever of you will be the chiefest, shall be servant of all" (Mark 10:44).

unto making utterances thus, they believe that evil is always found in much words.

"In the multitude of words there wanteth not sin: but he that refraineth his lips is wise" (Prov. 10: 19).

Hannah was very careful in her response to Eli the Priest responsible for services in the altar at that time. She was not rude and that attracted God's blessing from the same mouth that abused her publicly. **Opinion of others**: A humble person allows others to air their views before ruling off the matter. The belief is that theirs may be better than his own opinion when he hears a better suggestion and allows the better one to stand to the benefit of all.

"Let nothing be done through words strife or vainglory; but in out he lowliness of mind let each wise esteem other better than themselves" (Philippians 2:3)

Good Testimony: In humility, the integrity of one is the much valued. He believes that he not has a name to protect. He hardly forgets his family history. He maintains a standard and would not want his identity to be dented because of ungodly profit.

Forgiveness to One Another: Humility gives you the enablement to forgive easily nomatter how hard the situationseems to be.

TRUE HUMILITY

Every person wants to be comprehensible in service; there is no humble person that engages in eye service. Never you claim being humble while you dodge to serve people when you go to any form of occasion, you will easily locate humble people due to their service.

VI. Disregard to Publicity: Jesus in His occasional sayingsreminds us that when you do anygood, simply see yourself asnothing. Humility is displayed in not talking any glory for the job well done. Rather, the worker ascribes it to God. He sees no great deal in making noise. When he offers help, he does it confidently by not trumpet in it neither does he expect appreciation. Learn to behave like Jesus Christ. You do attract enemies when you go ahead presenting yourself, as if without you nothing works out

VII Avoid hurting People: Humility does not in anyway hurtsomeone. 1Try to avoid being thecause of someone's downfall ordeath Instead of being offendedby them you better leave thematter in their favour.

VII. Choice of Words: Humble Antecedents tries to be self-Controlled, always very careful in greatly successful and even being the highest. Serious attention should be given to these portions:

"Do ye think that the scripture saith in vain, the spirit that dwelleth in us lusteth to envy" (James 4:5, Peter 5:5).

If actually God gives grace to the humble then being humble is the sure-way to becoming successful in life. The above bible references should help us have a clear biblical idea on humility.

It is common that people do define humility in terms of a person who does not think for himself or see himself as important; one who is very submissive and does not stand up for himself but allows himself to be tossed around. Such belief was addressed more than a century ago by Josh Billings (1815-1885) when he said,

"the more humble a man is before God the more he will get role roughshod".

However, humility best describes a godly posture of the heart. Godly humility is the opposite of pride. Humble people never have a low estimate of their importance or think themselves as insignificant. Godly humility starts when we have seen things as they really are and realize that God is the creator of the universe and the standard by which everything is measured or evaluated.

CHAPTER FIVE

HUMILITY, A LIFE BASED

MODEL

Humility is often mistaken as a character trait that represents weakness; it is rather, one of the critical signs of strength in an individual. Humility manifests best, when a leader or an individual is highly placed or with plenty abundance, than in low state or in a position of scarcity.

NOT A CHARACTER TRAIT

The immediate past American president Obama owned up to a mistake at a conference. He took responsibility of the dash in the "Affordable Care Act". It is rare to see presidents or highly placed individuals admit their mistakes. For a prominent person, a president of the number one country of the world to admit his wrong, points to an obvious undeniable humility innate in him.

The true measure of humility is its exercise; when a leader in power, he still grant operational freedom to his opponents (1 Sam 24: 6-8). David of the bible is a good reference to this. He refused to revenge on King Saul even though he had such opportunity to deal with him. God in His terms does not want us to demonstrate power on the weak and the defenseless.

Humility as life-based model can be seen in forms of National unity on big values and issues. It will move an association and our politics forward there by giving the both, a lasting legacy we would all be proud of. Nelson Mandela escaped from spending nearly his entire adult life in prison. At the end of apartheid regime that ensured his life incarceration, and though he emerged the president and a very prominent one for that matter, in South Africa; he never seized to preach the message of reconciliation than that of revenge.

RECONCILIATION RATHER THAN REVENGE

Nigeria as a federal state hasone of their best educatedpresident in the person of DrGoodluck Ebele Jonathan.Despite different stages ofpositions he climbed; he neverallowed any of those positions which was climaxed with presidency defy his humble virtue, thus, relinquished power in order to save the country from blood thirsty men, who wanted doing anything including plunging the country to another civil war, but for the humility of Dr. Goodluck Ebele Jonathan. He demonstrated this rare Christian value by placing a high regard on human life and handed power over to the hungry maniacs, adding that the unity of Nigeria is valued than his own life. According to the bible:

"Likewise, ye younger, submit yourselves unto the elder. Yea, all of you be subject one to another, and be clothed with humility: for God resisteth the proud, and giveth grace to the humble" (1 Pt 5:5-7).

We can determine to live in humility and then be ready to receive God's blessing. Humility from Jesus model as seen in His life is the ability to be without pride or arrogance. This singular character should be lived by all his followers including you out there.

DONT MISS OUT: King Solomon in the book of proverbs gave warnings to thosewho refused to be humble. TheNew Testament is full of blessingsfor those who put others beforethemselves. You will definitelymiss out on the blessed abundantlife that God have for you if yourefuse to let go pride and followHis purpose for your life.

Humility is always measured in terms of belief and submission to

God's will if we miss this assertion, we will not be able to recognize humility when we see it. This is because humility occurs in the heart of a person, it is not the typical of the "flesh".

The clearest indicator of true humility is always misunderstood even by Christians and the world. of Jesus is the model of humility; He set the pace for meekness; He is the clearest picture of humility in the bible. Indeed, in history, Jesus Christ Himself modeled godly humility.

He defined humility in terms putting the will of God before our own will (Phil 2:5-8). Evidences lead to that effect

"That thou mightest know the certainty of those things, wherein thou hast been instructed" (Luke 1:4-15).

Mary's lifestyle points to her humble heart and endeared her to God and opened her for favour; it was humility that made her the hand maiden of the Lord; humility made her a worshiper, psalmist and an adulator.

God took notice of her service and worship and decided to announce her. The nucleus of true humility is placing value on God's instruction and word, thus, the need for a continued spread of the gospel which has a prominent blessing.

God traces you whenever you are doing something pleasing to Him. The reward of humility doesn't know any boundary. It runs from one generation to the next.

CHAPTER SX

HUMILITY AS A HONEY

Humility here is looked at from the view point of its value and usefulness to mankind (both high and low).

Socrates wrote that the unexamined life is not worth living. Humility helps us conduct an intense form of self-example and it is one principle that applies to the most important things in life, like, relationships, marriage, parenting, family and service; it is also a principle that can help individuals as well as businesses, governments and entire societies.

Humility is an indirect pointer to a person of wisdom; it is always easy to notice a fool and a

Humility As A Honey

braggart in the crowd, but the humble associated with his wisdom is lowly enough to be silent.

The humble is scarcely found; that means that humility is itself a scarce commodity: its scarcity is as a result of the benefits and values contained in it, thereby demanding a high price due to its importance. The sweetness is what we and the people around us enjoy when we produce and portray humility in our lives.

Finally, it is an antidote which fights and kills this deadly disease called pride in our lives. Let the Holy Spirit give us a full grip of the life of humility.

We Are Going To Expand This Lesson On These Points.

1. It attracts people.
2. Makes one wise.
3. Scarcely seen.
4. Attracts high price.
5. It is sweet.
6. It is medicinal.
7. Educating
8. Entertaining
9. Worthy of emulation
10. Makes one real

It is agreeable that honey attracts both humans and animals. There is this force that attracts people to you when you are humble, that is exactly what happened between Abraham and Lot his brother's son. Abraham heard God's voice and followed Him without a question or argument, Lot came into the scene by Abraham's complete obedience and became part of the promises. Abraham was not self- centered when he knew what the Lord had in stock for him, he allowed Lot to be part of it as he was attracted by the spirit of humility in the life of Abraham.

"Now the LORD had said unto Abram, Get thee out of thy country, and from thy kindred, and from thy father's house, unto a land that I will shew thee" (Gen 12:1-4).

The spirit of humility in a man attracts and allows others to take part and enjoy the blessings of God as a child of God.

Humility also attracts divine recognition and blessing as in Proverbs 22:4), By humility and the fear of God are riches, honor and life.

"Be of the same mind one toward another. Mind not high things, but condescend to men of low estate. Be not wise in your own conceits" (Rom 12:16).

It was the spirit of humility in him that made him arrive at wise conclusions, like not engaging into wars and battles with the neighboring countries which was quintessential with his father David. He maintained peace throughout his tenure of leadership, not staring up quarrels nor permit the blood thirsty men to drag him to war. Instead, he married a daughter from all the kings of his time, which sums 1,000.

True wisdom comes from God and is obtained by the spirit of humility in us

"Let no man deceive himself. f any man among you seemeth to be wise in this world, let him become a fool that he may be wise, For the wisdom of this world is foolishness with God. For it is written, He taketh the wise in their own craftiness" (1 Corinthians 3:18-19).

"In that hour Jesus rejoiced in spirit, and said, I thank thee, O Father, Lord of heaven and earth, that thou hast hid these things from the wise and prudent, and hast revealed them unto babes: even so, Father; for so it seemed good in thy sight" (Luke 10:21).

"A man's pride shall bring him low: but honor shall uphold the humble in spirit (Proverbs 29:23).

Humility attracts God's closeness, as seen in the book of

"The LORD is nigh unto them that are of a broken heart; and saveth such as be of a contrite spirit" (Psalm 34:18).

The prophet Isaiah 57:15 teaches us that when we humble ourselves before God and man, it draws God's presence closer to us. We are actually going to enjoy the full presence and closeness of God around and within our lives.

Honey, they say helps the brain to be bright, sharp and ***wise "Behold, I send you forth as sheep in the midst of wolves: be ye therefore wise as serpents, and harmless as doves" (Matt 10:16b).***

Here wisdom is attributed to heart harmlessness which is the be of a product of humility. In humility, these attributes emanates from the inside seen out ward in the life of any child of God. You will become wise in your dealings with man, it others in handling situations and loser to issues of life.

King Solomon for instance was humble and his humility made him wise. When God asked him "what do you want from me? His humble spirit guided him to be lowly and demanded wisdom than 'the mundane things of this world.

The original honey is not rampant; most of the ones we see here and there are artificially made. It is scarce because of its high quality which is useful to both high and low animals. Anything that produces honey must be very special and handled in a special way. In the world today what we see here and there is the smokescreen humility, the real or original humility is scarcely found in human beings. This is because it is of a high quality; it is one of the virtues inherent in Jesus Christ our Savior:

"Let this mind be in you, which was also in Christ Jesus, Who, being in the form of God, thought it not robbery to be equal with God, But

made himself of no reputation, and took upon A him the form of a servant, and was made in the likeness of men, And being found in fashion as a man, he humbled himself, and became obedient unto

death, even the death of here the cross" (Phil 2:5-8).

For anyone to have this is attribute he or she must be born again; he must accept Jesus in his or her life as a personal Lord and Savior. When this is done and is real or original, humility heritably sets in. And it should be lived out for people to see and benefit from it. Humility is peculiar to a particular set of people, hence, its scarceness.

Jesus in His ministry lived out this attribute:

"After that he poureth water into a basin, and began to wash the disciples' feet, and to wipe them with the towel wherewith he was girded", "Fear not, daughter of Zion: behold, thy King cometh, sitting on an ass's colt" (John 13:5, 12-15).

And the Lord wants us to follow His example by adopting the spirit of humility; that will enable us serve one another. This inherent quality will attract high demand, that is, people will be going here and there to look for us because we are carrying the attribute of God and Christ our Savior.

The quality, importance, usefulness and scarcity of original honey make its price to be high. Anything that has real value in it attracts high demand and price (said the economists). Jesus Christ our savior in His ministry here on earth, was able to possess this powerful virtue. He was obedient to His father, to the word of God, to human beings as a servant, even unto death.

"Let this mind be in you, which was also in Christ Jesus, Who, being in the form of God, thought it not robbery to be equal with God, But made himself of no reputation, and took upon him the form of a servant, and was made in the likeness of men, And being found in fashion as a man, he humbled himself, and became obedient unto death, even the death of the cross" (Philippians 2:5-8).

Because of this, God lifted Him high and gave Him a name which is higher than every other name

"Wherefore God also hath highly exalted him, and given him a name

which is above every name, That at the name of Jesus every knee should bow, of things in heaven, and things in earth, and things under the earth And that every tongue should confess that Jesus Christ is Lord, to the glory of God the Father" (Phil 2:9-1 1).

In the same manner, if we can adopt humility as a Lifestyle and be obedient to God our Father, to the word of God as we hear and read it, to humanity as servants, even unto death, we can attain this great height which God Himself is going to place us and He will make us more honorable than others in the society. The height at which God places us will indicate our worth. As a chosen generation, a royal priesthood, peculiar people, a holy nation, far above rubies, white as snow, purchased by the blood of the highest God, etc.

"Humble yourselves therefore under the mighty hand of God, that he may exalt you in due time" (1 Pt 5:6).

The word of God commanded us to humble ourselves under the mighty hand of God and He will exalt us (Lift us high) in due time. In order words, at a set time in God's agenda, He will lift you high above your imagination, above your qualifications, above your equals, above your levels, above your ability, above your strength, above your environment and high above your family background. For he that is lifted high is above all. (John 3:31,)

"But let it be the hidden man of the heart, in that which is not corruptible, even the ornament of a meek and quiet spirit, which is in the sight of God of great price" 1 Peter 3:4.

The sweetness of honey is in its content. All the ingredients contained in the honey itself are what produce the sweet taste in it, which attracts all hands and mouth to it. Likewise the sweetness of a man is the virtues inherent in him. This includes: patience, gentleness, obedience, longsuffering, peace, joy, goodness, meekness, forbearing one another, happiness, purity, forgiveness, love, unity, caring, selflessness, and faithfulness as well as bearing one another's burden.

All these ingredient of humility in a man will bring out the sweetness in him. If we can live out these ingredients of humility in our lives, it will bring out the sweetness in us thereby attracting people of all races to us. In other words, people will be interested in having relationships with us, hold business transactions with us, come to us in time of need and encouragement, and associate with us

Christ in his life time and ministry was able to produce these ingredient in Him by condescending to a servant instead of a Lord.

"For whether is greater, he that sitteth at meat, or he that serveth? Is not he that sitteth at meatP But I am among you as he that serveth" (Luke 22:27).

Going from place to place on foot, visiting people's houses, interacting with them one on one,

touching them and allowing them to touch Him even the woman with the issue of blood (Mark 5:25-27; Mark 10:44-45). Al these brought out the sweetness in Him and made people from all over the world to come looking for him.

Honey on the other hand is also medicinal: it cures various diseases and sickness in the life and body of human beings as well as animals. Humility as an attribute of Christ found in a child of God is also medicinal, in the sense that it fights against the spirit of pride in our lives.

When we allow the spirit of humility to dominate our lives, the spirit of pride will be nowhere to be found. With the spirit of humility in us, we cannot be high minded.

"Be of the same mind one toward another. Mind not high things, but condescend to men of low estate. Be not wise in your own conceits" (Romans 12:1 6).

We cannot despise others (Rom 14:2-3). We do not fight nor esteem ourselves better than others.

"In meekness instructing those that oppose themselves; if God peradventure will give them repentance to the acknowledging of the truth" (2 Timothy 2:25).

All these and many more are the product of pride which the spirit of humility in us fights against and brings us into God's hand where we become safe from such anomalies.

Whatever negative lifestyle we did not overcome will find a way to defeat us; Pride is a thief, a killer and a destroyer; we must therefore guard our minds with all diligence. We must as a matter of urgency, give adequate attention by applying the right antidote to destroy it. The evil we failed to uproot will likely, take deeper root to take a dangerous advantage of us

"Take us the foxes, the little foxes that spoil the vines: for our vines have tender grapes". (Song 2:15).

In pride, David took a census of his kingdom to see how great he was, though he repented and sought for mercy (2 Samuel 24:2-4, 8-10), yet, the damage has been already done. I acknowledge my sin that thou mightiest be justified when thou speakest (Psalm 51:1-4).

Self-righteous Job humbled himself, confessed that he was vile and repented (Job 40:1-5, 42:1-6).

King Nebuchadnezzar humbled himself and confessed that only God was great (Daniel 4:33-35, 37).

Wicked king Ahab humbled himself before God, so God did not bring judgment during his lifetime (1 Kings 21:17, 25-29).

Hezekiah humbled himself from the pride of his heart so that the wrath of the Lord came not (2 Chronicles 3:18). Lastly, the sacrifices of God are a broken spirit, a broken and a contrite heart, O God, thou wilt not despise.

"The sacrifices of God are a broken spirit: a broken and a contrite heart, O God, thou wilt not despise" (Psalms 51:17).

CHAPTER SEVEN

HUMILITY SAFETY PACK

Christians generally should be the most humble people on earth. It is absolutely right to humble yourself in the sight of God even to our seniors respectively. The crises ridden society we find our self, draws ones attention to the need for concrete humility.

"Likewise, ye younger, submit yourselves unto the elder. Yea, all of you be subject one They to another, and be clothed with humility: for God resisteth the proud, and giveth grace to the humble. Humble yourselves therefore under the mighty hand of God, that he may exalt you in due time: Casting all your care upon him; for he careth for you" (1Peter 5: 5-7).

MUCH ASSURANCE

There is much assurance of safety in humility. No matter how successful you are, safety is the number one life security you should earnestly contend for. This is true in the sense that safety by humility gives you sufficient protection. A promising country achieves safety of the citizens above every other thing. They do this by setting up security department across the state.

In the transport industries for instance: Road safety is usually set up to manage road hazards on National highways. This is intended to reduce casualties. In the same vein, there is security associated with the grace of God, when humility is uncompromisingly discerned in ones everyday attitude and behaviours.

There is much grace attached to humility because you receive favour from God as mankind even when you did not merit it. Therefore, humility becomes instrumental to the safety of lives and property.

AWARENESS OF GOD'S INFINITE GREATNESS

We should be humble because we have come to the awareness of God's infinite greatness as well as our own unworthiness. Indeed there is safety in humility while pride comes before a fall. According to Charles Spurgeon, ***"If you and I empty ourselves, depend on it, And God will fill us."***

Divine grace seeks to fill a vacuum, make a vacuum for it by being humble and God will fill that vacuum by His love.

"For I know the thoughts that I think toward you, saith the LORD, thoughts of peace, and not of evil, to give you an expected end" (Jeremiah 29:11).

Do we need more reasons for being humble than this? Who would want God to resist him/her? I do not wish to go against God in any way. I do not safety in humil ity wish to confront God with stubbornness, rebellion or pride. The only thing I need and which I strongly desire is grace; I need to receive as much grace as possible.

“But he giveth more grace. Wherefore he saith, God resisteth the proud, but giveth grace unto the humble" (James 4:6).

This could be the reason in (Luke 19) Jesus cautioned Zacchaeus the tax collector to come down from the sycamore tree. He suspended all program of the day and proceeded to the home of the very short man but humble man. Jesus can do something in your life even as you are going through this book. Haughtiness brings one to God's solid resistance; pride ushers one to the broad gate of absolute disgrace and ace humiliation; but Greater humility gives one greater grace and more opportunity before God. God's testimony of Job confirms the above assertion;

"And the LORD said unto in Satan, Hast thou considered my servant Job, that there is none like him in the earth, a perfect and an upright man, one that feareth God, and escheweth evil? (Job 1:8).

Is it not good for one's humility brings him/her a good testimony before God, to the extent of calling him/her MY SERVANT? This certifies that humility draws you closer to God and draws God closer to you.God fought a great fight for Moses; not because he cannot fight for himself, but because Moses was too humble to raise his voice on anyone who confronts him. The scripture said that; Moses has no equal in meekness, faithfulness and humbleness.

"My servant Moses is not so, who is faithful in all mine house. With him will I speak mouth to mouth, even apparently, and not in dark speeches; and the similitude of the LORD shall he behold: wherefore then were ye not afraid to speak against my servant Moses (Numbers 12: 7,8).

He can promote you as He deemed fit.

"Humble yourselves in the sight of the Lord, and he shall lift you up" (James 4:10).

The captivating side of the whole thing is the assurance of lifting up the humble. If you need God's special grace for exploit in a noticeable proportion, it then calls for your being evidently humble in God's presence. How can one claim to be a Christian when there is no evidence of humility in him? How can say you are born again without the presence of humility? If you are a child of God, there must be humility in you because Jesus Christ first humbled himself, and any person who has the Spirit of Christ in him/her will definitely possess the mind of Christ which is characterized with humility.

"Let this mind be in you, become which was also in Christ Jesus' to the (Philippians 2:5).

There is no wrong in possessing the mind of Christ; it is not a crime to possess the Spirit of Christ; the scripture said that it will not be counted against you as robbery. Jesus Christ exhibited humility when He chose not to align Himself with God-state but the lowered Himself like human. When you pattern yourself in this form, story will tell itself in the shortest period of time. Word

STEPS TO DEVELOP HUMILITY

The extent you have gone so far enjoying this substance have sensitized you to pursue humility.

The hard nut to crack is: "How can one develop a humble lifestyle.

This particular part encourages that the possibility to become one is sure. It is as getting to the storebuilding which requires gradual climbing of the staircase before you know it you are already in the first floor and subsequent floors you might desire.

1. Meditate on the credibility of God: He is the King of kings, the Lord of lords and the One the angels tremble at His feet. Controls all things and sustains the universe by the power of His word. There is no one as glorious as He is.

2. Reflect on your sins against Him and unbelievable

(James 1:17). ..."A man can say receive nothin8, except it be God given him from heaven" (John 3:27). God's credibility has made available every strength and skill so if one is not careful, God can only remove either without consulting anybody. On this ground, you should simply go on your knee or prostrate before Him.

6. Make bare your sins and temptations before Him:

Nothing is so quite like humbly admitting your weaknesses. When you apply this, you are simply indicating that you need God's mercy.

7. Be fast to listen and slow to speak: Proud people always want to dish out ideas, opinions and thoughts. The humble person in contrast listens to what others say and recognize the fact that God can give a spiritual gift to anyone.

8. Don't be Mr. Right: God cautioned Elijah that he is not the only righteous man on earth. (1 Kings 18:2224) Solomon added in (Eccl 7:16) that one should not be over-righteous. The truth is only God knows all things. In fact, we undoubtedly know that we can only boast of little knowledge. Therefore, to consider are that we are always right is both pride and stupidity. Humble yourself my friend before the Lord by admitting either that you do not know or could be wrong

9. Express Appreciation: Appreciation is an expressionthat you are the recipient of many mercy He poured out on you: ***(Romans 5:8) "But God Ie commendeth his love toward us, in that, while we were yet sinners, Christ died for us".***

This overwhelming reality should cause you to humble yourself before God. You are a perfect sinner and living against the that living God and yet He fix all your sins on Christ so that you could but know Him.

3. Think of your human Frailty: My dear, your every ever breath, heartbeat, sensory organs and mental health are all from God. He can stop them from functioning at anytime (Psalm 90)

"Says that our lives are like dust here today and disappears tomorrow".

4. Recall your full inability to control a simple thing in this life: If you want to be humbled before the Lord, think on the fact that you cannot ultimately control your heartbeat, the blessings and challenges you the encounter including your finances. We can take actions that have certain consequences but God controls every part of our lives.

5. All is from God: Realize that every good thing, talent and gifts is from God which He has the power to withdraw. ***"Every good gift and every perfect gift is from above, and cometh down from the Father of lights, with whom is no variableness, neither shadow of***

turning" gifts from God. You did not earn or merit either of the gifts that are operational in you. The whole thing is just that God so much loves you ***(John 3:16) "For God so loved the world, that he gave his only begotten Son, that whosoever believeth in him should not perish, but have everlasting life".***

10. You cannot be ignored: This is more along the lines of(Psalm 90) which calls us toremember our days. Your personis dispensable. Not everywhere and in everything you are valued.You are not essential that withoutyou nothing works. When it Comes to God's system, if one diesnow the church will continue thegate of hell cannot stop the operation. Knowledge of these single facts will turn you down to humble lifestyle.

11. Busy on others: Do you realize that the thing that bothers you about others may even be what you do as well. Sometimes, you excessively practice such acts than the people you are correcting. Jesus in (Matt 7; 5) spoke of removing the spake on your eyes in order to see clearly to help others. You should work on yourself first. Paul in his writing ***(1 Corinthians 12:3) ""Wherefore I give you to understand, that no man speaking by the Spirit of God calleth Jesus accursed: and that no man can say that Jesus is the Lord, but by the Holy Ghost".*** We should examine ourselves.

12. Pray non-stop, Pray: Prayer is the key; we commune with God through this channel When you pray, you are simply telling God that you cannot make it without Him. Prayer is the hush it declaration of weakness and a verbal acknowledgment that you are need God's sustaining grace. But when you neglect prayers, you are unwittingly declaring that you are over-strong, and do not need divine help.

13. Ask for Help: When you seek the prayers and help of others, it is an act of humility. You are admitting that they have knowledge and insight that you do not have. Such will save time for you to do other things.

14. Applaud Others: This particular one is exigent; this is so because people tend to themselves being associated with good things in order to be a reference point; than seeing it happen for others. Humility sees it in another way, in that, one is expected to be happy when others are honored or favored. The Holy writs said, ***"Be kindly affectioned one to another with brotherly love; in honour preferring one another" (Rom 12:8-21).*** God delights in you when you applaud the good things in others.

15. Focus on the cross of Christ: Focusing on Christ's cross takes you to higher level of morality. Nothing should make us humble like the perfect sinless son of

God willingly pouring out His life to rescue those who never acknowledged him, people who hated Him and rebelled against Him. At the cross, the glorious Son of God died so that you could receive eternal life and joy in Him. We should in fact humble ourselves because it honors God. Christ Jesus humbled Himself; so humility is critical in the service and worship of God. In the vanguard of Christian lives, remains an essential character.

16. Be Real: Make yourself real before others, and never lift yourself up. Do not act as a chameleon.

CHAPTER EIGHT

BUSINESS SUCCESS

Humility if adopted as a path in business, it will cause you to celebrate. Though majority in this field have failed to acknowledge that if you are humble, you can still make it. They believe that business success must be mixed with schemes on their client. When you are honest and God fearing, the possibility to make it gradually is obvious.

In fact, it still turns out that the quality we should all be striving for in these uncertain unpredictable times is not hubris but it's opposite. True humility as aforementioned "possesses a modest view of one's own importance".

THE STRENGTH OF HUMILITY

This mindset can be a powerful asset to this task changing business life. Humility holds an accurate and realistic view of their product and organization. It allows honest assessment of what has gone well and what has not. And it creates a conical openness to positive change. This mindset of humility helps you to start with a lean start up.

"For I know the thoughts that I think toward you, saith the LORD, thoughts of peace, and not of evil, to give you an exxpected

end" (Jeremiah 29:11).

Many beggarly individuals have ever remained on same landscape due to the mindset of waiting until huge capital is raised and attractive environment is acquired. They fail to acknowledge that time flies and capability diminishes, opportunities may not be exactly the same even if it reappears.

In the country, if you do not heat it hard, the cash at hand might disappear because money has wings,

"Wilt thou set thine eyes upon that which is not? For riches certainly make themselves wings; they fly away as an eagle toward heaven' (Proverbs 23: 5).

Other circumstances may show up to demoralize you. The power of humility has ever remained constant and states that 'one should start with what he has and where he is'. It is advisable that you better start small and then grow greater.

"And Jesus increased in wisdom and stature, and in favour with God and man" (Luke 2:52).

Better Ideas Can Come From Anywhere And

ANY DAY

Idea is what every beginner need; while humility allows wonderful idea to flow into you. Closest sampling can be done within a round table meeting with friends or employees. On this note you listen to several super opinions, scan them closely and pick the relevant ones for use. Even when the leader or manager finds it difficult to follow the laid down principles, it demands that you lay your pride aside and admit that no one has all the answers needed for a successful business. In as much as you want success in the business, you need the idea of people in both the higher and lower echelons. Consequently, the way to achieve and get things done is undermine the thought of who gets the credit.

WELCOME FAULT: The Holy book, the Bible points out encompassing crucialinformation:

"Confess your faults one to another, and pray one for another, that ye may be healed. The effectual fervent prayer of a righteous man availeth much' (James 5:16).

The above scripture instructs that we confess our mistakes with the very affected persons. You demonstrate humility in practice by neglecting shame and admit your wrongs. Take the responsibility of your actions, the Netflix boss, Reed Husting demonstrated this when he made a sincere public apology for a sudden hike in price on their products, he said "I messed up". "I owe everyone an explanation in hindsight; I slid into arrogance based on past success" he concluded.

Admitting errors benefits and builds trust amongst employees and customers. So with the above explanation, every legitimate fear should be let go for the good of the expected business success.

MODIFYING CHANNELS: Actually, drawing from the strength of humility in successpreferably in all humanendeavors implies on thefollowing.

PAUSE AND REFLECT: It is always important tolook back on what worked andwhat did not work, identifyingways to improve in the future.

Hire and from diverse teams create chances where constructive criticisms can spring up. Bring together people from a wide range of background, skill, settings and perception.

INVEST IN INSIGHTS; Put your own opinion down first. Balance it with the opinion of others and take the best option.

BE AN EXAMPLE: Be open and humble; thiswill allow both the employees andcustomers to think for a way forward to success.

CHAPTER NINE

WHEN GOD IS ALLOWED

In chapter two, I indicated that God is not man. He lifts up and humbles. Hannah got it right when God proved Himself God, by causing an outburst of change through lifting Hannah from the dustbin to Dynasty:

"And Hannah prayed, and said, My heart rejoiceth in the LORD, mine horn is exalted in the LORD: my mouth is enlarged over mine enemies; because I rejoice in thy salvation. There is none holy as the LORD: for there is none beside thee: neither is there any rock like our God. Talk no more so exceeding proudly; let not arrogancy come out of your mouth: for the LORD is a God of knowledge, and by him actions are weighed (arrogancy: Heb. Hard) The bows of the mighty men are broken, and they that stumbled are girded with strength. They that were full have hired the out themselves for bread; and and they that were hungry ceased: so that the barren hath born seven; and she that hath many children is waxed feeble. The LORD killeth, and maketh alive: he bringeth down to the grave, and bringeth up. The LORD maketh poor, and maketh rich: he bringeth low, and ifteth up. He raiseth up the poor out of the dust, and lifteth up the beggar from the dunghill, to set them among princes, and to make them inherit the throne of glory: for the pillars of the earth are the LORD'S, and he hath set the world upon them (1Samuel 2: 1-8). **LIFESTYLE OF HUMILITY**

Something of the same nature happened to Zacharias in (Luke 1:63-75); he appreciated God for considering him worthy of witnessing the fulfillment of the age-long prophecy:

"And he asked for a writing table, and wrote, saying, His name is John. And they marveled all And his mouth was opened immediately, his tongue loosed, and he spake, and praised God And fear came on all that dwelt round about them: and all these sayings were noised abroad throughout all the hill country of Judaea. And all they that heard them laid them up in their hearts, saying, what manner of child shall this be! And the hand of the Lord was with him. And his father Zacharias was filled with the Holy Ghost, and prophesied, saying, Blessed be the Lord God of Israel for he hath visited and redeemed his people, and hath raised up an horn of salvation for us in the house of his servant David; As he spake by the mouth of his holy prophets, which have been since the world began: That we should be saved from *When God Is Allowed* ***our enemies, and from the hand of all that hate us To perform the mercy promised to our fathers, and to remember his holy covenant; The oath which he sware to our father Abraham, that he would grant unto us, that we being delivered out of the hand of our enemies might serve him without fear, in holiness and righteousness before him, all the days of our life" (Luke 1: 63-75).***

Furthermore, God expect all His children alike to live a lifestyle of humility. Failure to work on yourself while He is patient with you will result to a shameful humiliation.

God directs a severe corrective measure on the recalcitrant as a mark of love to all His dear children in-order to devour to restore them. Parents and Teachers engage this method when a child played down on a given instruction during school hours or at home. The very child then faces two options: either to take the punishment or to drop from school. The scripture according to Proverbs persuades parents to whip the child for the purpose of bringing them up to decent living before they get out of hand.

Disgracing The Grace

Apostle Paul warned us equally about the danger resulting joking with the grace of Christ,

"For if we sin wilfully after that we have received the knowledge of the truth, there remaineth no more sacrifice for sins, But a certain fearful looking for of judgment and fiery indignation, which shall devour the adversaries" (Hebrews 10:26, 27).

Many people will find their way to hellfire due to erroneous conviction that God will not destroy this beautiful earth; and that He will change His mind later, since He is a Loving Father.

The "Born Again" equally stands on this ground to excuse theirselves that if He did not punish them on past sins, He will equally do nothing as they continue in same likely ungodliness. God, having seen persistency of man's inglorious behaviour and evil practices, declared:

"He that is unjust, let him be unjust still: and he which is filthy, let him be filthy still: reduce and he that is righteous, let him be righteous still: and he that is holy, let him be holy God's still" (Rev 22:11).

NOT A WEAKLING Does the above scripture by quotation suggest that God is a weakling? Not, at all. He will into definitely deal with all forms of totally ungodliness of people. The best thing to do is to return like the prodigal son before it becomes too even late. I give you this assurance; He will celebrate you because He cannot lie, neither is He afraid of any person.

"He restoreth my soul: he leadeth me in the paths of righteousness for his name's sake" (Psalm23:3)

God humbles a person to reduce His dignity and pride. He equally can prepare them for advanced usefulness. Receiving God's correction can be seen in His dealings with the Israelites [1Cor 10:1-12]. He delivered them by great miracles. Then led them into a barren wilderness and totally humbled them.

After 430 years of slavery the Israelites had given up hope of even knowing freedom and possessing their own land. Then a prophet Moses appeared among them preaching hope. He went from field to field and house to house telling them:

"I have seen your affliction" (Deuteronomy 7:6-8) "And the children of Israel said unto them, Would to God we had died by the hand of the LORD in the land of Egypt, when we sat by the flesh pots, and when we did eat bread to the full for ye have brought us forth into this wilderness, to kill this whole assembly with hunger" (Exodus 16:3).

They played with God and He taught them the lesson of their lives, (1 Cor 10:6, 11).

"And he humbled thee, and suffered thee to hunger, and fed thee with manna, which thou knewest not, neither did thy fathers knou that he might make thee know that man doth not live by bread only, but by every word that procedeth out of the mouth of the LORD doth man live" (Deuteronomy 8:3).

God humbled them and also dealt with Pharaoh who refused to let go of His people.

THE BEST FOR YOU

If we refused to humble ourselves, it implies that we are challenging God the creator of all. It is best that you humble yourself instead of God humbling you. He might use any choice of instrument to humiliate you. God can do it anywhere or anyhow. You cannot serve Him a letter of cost.People do not care to know your pains, sad mood, ill health, killers and disgrace but will only notice your mistakes. This of assertion came up due to my recent experience in ministry, the where I was assigned to a virgin land, (to plough and to cultivate) which involves numerous toils in the kingdom business.

Many concluded that I will not survive it. Humanly speaking, it was an impossible task but Good spoke to me that this is the time to learn humility; He may have seen me then as His vegetable servant.

Look, when we stand at the judgment seat, we will not be judged because on healings we performed, demons we casted out, development we made at our positions, rather, we will be judged considering our level of dependence on and obedience to His word and His will.
The next inclusive in the list of those directly humiliated by God was "LUCIFER" as shown in the book of Ezekiel 14. He was the next after the trinity but eventually opposed God by his pride, which earned him enthronement. Today he stands as a reference in the black list of those that refused to humble self.

Adam and Eve fell in the same category; they were very comfortable in the exclusive garden without any experience of harsh condition of life. They saw no reason to consider humility as a requisite of fellowshipping with God. They created a chance for query; He is almighty. He (God) never masterminds both individuals as mac and nations respectively. It is possible to demonstrate with some supernatural power and yet knew not leaning wholly upon the Lord. This could make Him to strip us of prove all confidence and destroy all that remains of selfrighteousness, spiritual pride and boastings.

He humbles all who are destined to inherit His great spiritual blessings. Just imagine how He apprehended the usual Saul o Tarsus, a self-confident walk man who was consumed with full knowledge of the scriptures, very zealous and made him blind on the fateful day. Saul had to be humiliated before the entire me world. To God the reason for the humiliating him and others was never in doubt. He carried it out as made clear in

"Who fed thee in the wilderness with manna, which thy fathers knew

not, that he might humble thee, and that he might prove thee, to do thee good at thy latter end" (Deut 8:16).

In order to humble him furthermore, Paul being led around like a child and waiting helplessly for few days learnt his lessons, so that he no longer walks with high shoulders.

Based on my personal experiences in ministry, the attitude of some people towards me has helped me develop an excellent spirit in humility, thereby prioritizing heaven at all satan to interact with them And they gave in to his antics. They were promised that if you eat the forbidden fruit, you would look like the Omniscience. This frame of mind, the destructive suggestion of the devil, carried them away. Their divine placement was no longer comfortable to them. The aftermath was that they were expelled from the celebrated atmosphere.

Why should you not stay under your leader, parent, boss and master? Why should you not humble yourself and place under the ones that have the rule over you? Why should you permit pride and arrogance to rub you of the rest of heaven?

There is time for everything. Those that remain humble and finished well, were they not settled by their master? Stop looking for short-cuts to greatness. Christ had similar challenges and temptations, but humility made Him to resist the three Greek gifts of Satan. At last, He is being celebrated forever.

CHAPTER TEN

HUMILITY FRAME WORK

Quotes

It is very obvious that we are not equal; there are some who have acquired higher and detailed knowledge on certain issues than you. Most of them are dead but are immortalized by the works they kept in national archives, libraries or museums. The following amongst other numerous authorities can steer us to desire nothing better than a humble lifestyle not minding the misrepresentations.

Humility is crucial to real success; many people became successful in wealth but lose their character. Success is not what you get, but what you become as a person. It was pride that changed angels into devils, it is humility that transformed humans into angels.

1. Pride makes us artificial while humility makes

us real-**Saint Augustine.**

2. There is no respect for others without

humility in one's self-**Thomas Merton.**

3. The greatest friend of truth is time, her

greatest enemy is prejudice, and her

constant Companion is humility-**Hari Frederic**

Amiel. 4. Selflessness is humility. Humility and freedom go hand in hand. Only a humble person can be free- **Charles Caleb Colton.**

5. The most wonderful weapon to defeat the devil is humility. For he does not know how to employ it, neither does he know how to defend himself from it-**Jeff Wilson.**

6. He who offers a whole offering shall be rewarded with a whole offering. He who offers a burnt offering shall be rewarded for a burnt offering. But he who offers humility, to God and being money shall be rewarded with a reward of as if he had offered all the sacrifice in the world- **Vincent the Paul.**

7. Humility is not thinking less of yourself it's thinking yourself less- **Rick Warren.**

8. Humility is not a character trait to develop. It's the natural byproduct of being with Jesus- **Louie** 9. I believe the first test of a truly great man in his**humility-John Ruskin.**

10. Do you wish to rise? Begin by descending. You plan a tower that will pierce the clouds? Lay first the foundation of humility **Saint Augustine.**

11. They would tell us to seek money, power, and success. God tells us to seek humility, service and love- **Pope Francis.**

12. Nothing sets a person so much out of the devils reach than humility-**Jonathan Edwards.**

13. Plenty of people wish to become devout but no one wishes to be humble-**La Rochefoa Cauld..**

14. Humility is nothing but truth, and pride is nothing but it is still but lying

15. Never look down on anybody unless you are helping them up- **Jesse Jackson.**

16. Humility of heart is the first step to salvation**Lac Poonen.**

17. Only humility knows how to appreciate and admire the good qualities of others-**Sir**

CONCLUSION

Many people have a very poor understanding about humility. This is the main reason why they have not developed it though they may have desired it but it is still far from them. As God may have it, this book has touched the term humility from its grassroots to the peak, pinpointing service as a therapy for mediocrity to all persons alike.

Peradventure you desire a quick glance at the books contents I believe this conclusive part will capture and satisfy your quest.

Being humble is not groveling in front of others or thinking that they are no good and others are better than you. That is not what I am expressing. Rather, when you are humble, you are free from pride and arrogance. You know that inside you, you are not derisory; to rather, you know who you are in Christ.

You therefore do not need to defend yourself when you acknowledge what the Bible says about Humility. When you know your position in Christ, you can be a peacemaker with no need of fight for your rights; you can walk humbly in the power of the Holy Spirit and no longer in your strength.

The picture of humility in the bible is one of a strong person who loves others, and never someone who is a wimp according to

"Let nothing be done through strife or vainglory; but in lowliness of mind let each esteem other better than themselves" (Philippians 2:3).

Humility will feel your brain to know that you need God's help in everything. You also know that you cannot succeed on your strength. It persuades you to continue giving thanks to God for your talents and gifts including accomplished.

Humility has never been taken to be weak or passive.

"A soft answer turneth away Wrath: but grievous words stir up anger" (Proverbs 15:1).

If you are humble, you can handle unfair treatment that rains on you like stones without Road being bitter about it.

Godly humility entails that you do not be overtaken by revenge on provocations (Ephesians 4:31- 32). In addition, you do not need to put a "False front" to show your humility.

The better you know God, the less you have to prove it. Meanwhile, the last topic before this conclusion on frame quotes should dare you to give hot chase to proud lifestyle hence it will render you totally barren.

BIBLIOGRAPHY

David Books [2016] The Road To Character. House Trade, Walthern, MA, USA.

Edgar .H. Schein, 2013. HUMBLE ENQUIRY. Barrett- Koehier Publishers, Dallas, TX USA.

Dr Dereh Prince. [2016] PRIDE VERSEs HUMILITY. Whittaker House, Columbia, MD USA

Dr Charles Whitefield [2006] POWER OF HUMILITY. HCI

Jerry Brides [2016] BLESSING OF HUMILITY. Nav

Press Publishing, Columbia, MD USA.

Authorized King James Version, [1979] Holman Bible Publishers.

Revd Dr Anoweh V.A.P. [2014] NOT THE END OF THE ROAD, Anoweh V, Prints; 163 Tetlow Rd OW, Imo State, Nig.

ACKNOWLEDGMENT

I am grateful to my Father in heaven, who impels my mind to reach the world through this publication.

I give kudos to my immediate family members for understanding on my God's driven goal.

All my highly venerated friends are also acknowledged for their untimely support.

I acknowledge my sons in Christ who were there for me. Dr Sampson Obinali, Pastor George Best, Pastor Fedinand Nze, David Onyekachi; Elder Chidi Uzoechi and his wonderful Family. I will not forget Late Elder Chris Iwuji's family; Elder E, Uzowuru and

Engineer Chile.

I acknowledge my esteemed friends like: Pastor K.C Awuzie, Evang. Uche Adimoha, Pastor Louis Okereafor, H.R.H Barnabas Obirieze, Rev. Dr J. Okere Ewendu and Bishop Major Chukwukereuba.

Special thanks to all Pastors and members of Orlu North District of Holiness Evangelistic Church.

www.ingramcontent.com/pod-product-compliance
Lightning Source LLC
LaVergne TN
LVHW050342160826
845677LV00014B/3751

* 9 7 9 8 3 5 1 7 8 1 9 4 5 *